Thoughts On Grief

My Journey Through The Grief Process

Christina (Chris) Hunter

Thoughts On Grief—My Journey Through The Grief Process

By: Christina (Chris) Hunter

Copyright Pending 2024 © by Christina Hunter

This publication may not be reproduced, stored in an electronic system, or transmitted in any form or by any means, electronic, mechanical, photocopy, recording, or otherwise, without proper credit to the author. Brief quotations may be used without permission.

Most Scripture quotations are from the King James Version Bible.

Scripture quotations marked (NIV) are taken from the Holy Bible, New International Version®, NIV®. Copyright © 1973, 1978, 1984, 2011 by Biblica, Inc.™ Used by permission of Zondervan. All rights reserved worldwide. www.zondervan.comThe "NIV" and "New International Version" are trademarks registered in the United States Patent and Trademark Office by Biblica, Inc.™

Woodsong Publishing, Seymour, IN

ISBN 978-1-961482-10-4

Table Of Contents

Foreword
Introduction
Backstory
Preface
Chapter 1: Our Love Story - He Gives and He Takes Away
Chapter 2: The First Month
Chapter 3: Sorrows Like Deep Billows Roll
Chapter 4: Painful "Happy Events"
Chapter 5: Reality – The Six-Month Mark
Chapter 6: The Chair – To Sit or Not to Sit?
Chapter 7: Your Grieving Children and Grandchildren
Chapter 8: Keep Moving
Chapter 9: Making Progress on Your Journey
Chapter 10: Choices
Chapter 11: Sweet Remembrance of Those Last Days
Chapter 12: Whatever Thy Hands Find to Do
Chapter 13: Caregiver Role Strain
Chapter 14: Summary of Thoughts – Still Everything

Foreword

True empathy for those who have felt the relentless sting of grief is unfortunately only earned by experience. With a beautiful mixture of facts and feelings, Chris Hunter takes us on a personal journey of good days and bad ones. Her book does not prove to be the ultimate authority, but it gives hope to every reader who suffers from the pain of loss by reminding us all that God is still in control and moving forward is an option. I'm sad she has this story to tell, but I'm thankful that God has allowed her to share it with us.

Pastor Joshua B Carson
Senior Pastor / Calvary Tabernacle

Introduction

Hi, I'm Chris. I grew up in south central rural Indiana in a conservative Christian home with a great, uneventful childhood. I was the second child to a very young couple who married as teens and had their first two of five children before three years of marriage. I can say I lived a "sheltered" life without any childhood trauma and had no idea the events that my adult life would bring. I've often said I am thankful that God does not let us see our future, because I would have not been able to comprehend it.

I married, the first time, at the young age of eighteen. My marriage was not anything like what I had observed in my home with my family, and that is when my "life events" began. I was divorced four years later, at twenty-two years of age with a two-year-old child with disabilities. I remember the Scripture that God gave me shortly after this traumatic event, which states "Wherefore seeing we also are compassed about with so great a cloud of witnesses, let us lay aside every weight, and the sin which doth so easily beset us, and let us run with patience the race that is set before us" (Hebrews 12:1). I'm not sure I fully understood what that verse meant, and little did I know that the race had just begun and that my whole life would be running this race. I saw so many friends and acquaintances around me walk away from God due to circumstances similar to mine, but I knew that I had made a covenant with God at a very early age, and I would not walk away. Because of that, Christ has not walked away from me, and He has kept His promises to me. I have had other heartbreaking circumstances in my life, but I have held fast to what I know – my trust must lie in Him and Him only, and I will overcome anything that comes my way by His mercy and grace.

I have been told for years by the few that know most of my life story that I needed to write a book. I had talked about writing a book on "restoration" and as years and life passed, I just could not find the right time. There was always another life situation of restoration that could be added to the book. Becoming a young divorcee at the age of twenty-two, and now, this most current compound grief experience and widow at the age of fifty-nine, finally propelled me to sit down and write. Some may think that maybe I feel this is the "end of my story," but I do not: I just feel the timing is right. I'm sure there will be more to my story, and the only reason I am here today to tell you about it so far is because of my covenant with God and His infinite faithfulness to me. What I do know is that He has led me through the wilderness time and time again, and He will do it once again on my grief journey. "I will bless the LORD at all times: his praise shall continually be in my mouth" (Psalm 34:1).

The Backstory

Hi, I'm Chris, and this is some of my story....

The first week of March 2020, the same week the COVID pandemic hit the country, I was working in New York City and was stuck in traffic on the interstate with coworkers when I received a text from my dad with results from a recent CT scan he had. I read through the CT scan, and a feeling of serious concern swept over me. Being a registered nurse (RN) for many years, I knew it was not a good report and my dad likely had pancreatic cancer – one of the worst types of cancers to be diagnosed with. It was to be confirmed by further testing and biopsy in the coming weeks.

I returned home a few days later as the country was reacting to the pandemic and was thankful to make it home. I had been traveling two to three weeks a month for the past several years due to the demands of my job with a government contractor who operates Job Corps centers for the Department of Labor (DOL). My travels came to a screeching halt when all travel was suspended as the country and DOL determined how they would handle the pandemic – another book could be written on this! I accompanied Dad and Mom to a few initial appointments, sometimes having to beg my way into doctors' offices and/or testing sites due to restrictions related to the pandemic protocols. It was confirmed that Dad had pancreatic cancer, and he began treatment right away. (He wrote a book about his journey through pancreatic cancer that you can read for more details from his perspective: "Finding God, My Journey Through Pancreatic Cancer" by Nick Seniour.)

Dad fought cancer rigorously and lived twenty-five months after asking God for "two years" to "get his house in order." Mom and I cared for him throughout his illness. In early November of 2021, nearing the end of Dad's journey, my husband (Max) had a CT scan, at my request due to him losing seventy pounds that year without much effort on his part and his blood sugar spiraling out of control despite the weight loss. After my dad's journey, and because I am an RN and could only think of the main function of the pancreas, I had asked Max to request his primary physician to order a scan just to assure there was not a concern with his pancreas. I remember the day I received the text from him with his CT scan results. I, again, was on a business trip and at a conference in Washington, D.C. It was Monday, November 15, 2021. When I read the scan results it was like reading my dad's results again. I was in shock and concerned. It was only Monday of the conference, and I had to make it through the week knowing there would be more definitive testing and treatment depending on the test results. It was another six weeks or so before we had a definitive diagnosis after MRIs and a biopsy. It was unbelievable, but my sixty-year-old husband had pancreatic cancer – the same diagnosis as my dad. The following week, it was confirmed that my dad's cancer had spread, and he was terminal. His surgeon told him he "may have until Easter," which was in mid-April that year. In January 2022 Max began his rigorous three months of chemotherapy treatments. It was a very difficult journey for him with horrible side effects. His treatments ended by the end of March. Dad had been in home hospice from the beginning of the year and was starting to rapidly decline. He passed away on Palm Sunday, April 10, 2022. His homegoing service was on Friday, April 15th, Good Friday, and Max and my 33rd wedding anniversary.

Max underwent the complex Whipple surgery to remove the cancer in his pancreas in mid-May, had complications, and was in the hospital thirteen days. He was finally able to come home on tube feedings and then recovered well at home. Due to the very negative way his body reacted to chemo pre-surgery, he chose to opt out of the six months of post-surgery treatment. We had a front row seat in my dad's journey, and he was very well aware of the likely results without divine intervention, but he decided to put the outcome in God's hands. He recovered from the surgery and had a great five to six months post-surgery until early November 2022 when I noticed he was jaundice and requested he go for lab work and another CT scan. There was no cancer in his pancreas, but it was in his liver and was so advanced that there were no options for treatment. He was in and out of the hospital for the next couple of weeks, stents placed, pain management, etc., and ended up coming home on hospice on November 29th. He was gone by December 11th, eight months after my dad passed away. He was sixty-one, and I was a widow at fifty-nine. It was devastating for me, our children, and young grandchildren.

Less than two months later (February 7, 2023), my

fifty-five-year-old brother was diagnosed with liver cancer and passed away on October 15, 2023. Three deaths of three men closely related to me within eighteen months. Interestingly, they all passed away on a Sunday. Most would say that this resulted in complex or complicated grief. Obviously, the loss of my dad and my brother are heartbreaking, and I often don't know exactly who I may be grieving the loss of, but my journey through grief discussed in this book is primarily about the loss of my husband, Max E. Hunter, August 29, 1961 – December 11, 2022. Throughout this book, I will include my "thoughts on grief" that I have journaled as I've walked (sometimes crawled) through the first year of my grief journey as well as other narratives that I feel may be helpful as I reflect on when the journal excerpts were written. My hope and prayer is that my expression of my journey may be helpful to you on your journey. Everyone's journey is different and cannot nor should not be compared, but you may find some similarities in my journey to yours.

Preface:

Journal Entry: The Process

December 11, 2021

Since we received the news that Max has a high probability of having pancreatic cancer, I have struggled with what I knew was coming. I have battled in my mind with the fact that I know I have faith in God and that He has this all in control but also struggled with what I know from being a nurse for many years and the most recent experience with my own dad and the journey he has been on for the past twenty-one months with pancreatic cancer. I have seen the miracles of God, I have experienced them myself from a young adult to my current, not so young, adult season that I am in. I have seen very recent miracles and situations worked out due to prayer and faithfulness.

Why do I now keep telling God "I believe but help my unbelief." Today I realized it's the process – the journey that you take to get to that miracle or to be on the other side of the challenge. It's kind of strange because in your younger years you have faith and, based on your beliefs, you know that things will turn out okay and, for me, I know that God is faithful, and He will have the final say. However, I realized why this newest need for a miracle hit me like a ton of bricks – it's the process. The process can be hard - I know it all too well. It can knock you to the ground (hopefully you land on your knees in prayer), and it can take a toll on you. However, I know through it all God will be walking beside us, guiding the doctors, and be in control of it all. No matter what the outcome I know He is faithful.

I have known His faithfulness through many challenges and heartbreaks throughout my life from a scandalous divorce at a very young age to injuries as an adult in which I had to learn to walk again, to incidents that pierced my heart by people very close to me, and what do I know about these times? I know that God was faithful, and He stayed very close to me on those journeys. Those are some of the most memorable times in my life in which I felt the closeness of God and had a peace that was beyond human understanding. With that said, I can only trust God and look forward to what will come from this journey that Max and I will be on, the process will be tough, but we will know, once again, the closeness and faithfulness of God.

Chapter 1

Our Love Story - He Gives and He Takes Away

I was a young divorcee with a four-year-old daughter when Max and I met at a wedding of a mutual friend. Several years before that I had gone through a terrible divorce and was betrayed and treated in a way that left me with very little trust in men and was not interested in putting my trust in another man only to be betrayed and wounded again. Max pursued me despite this, even telling his mom when we met (and had not even been on a date) that I was the girl he was going to marry. Long story short – we met in April 1988 and were married one year later in April of 1989. I always teased him that he got me from a "secondhand store."

In the thirty-three plus years of marriage we built a family (a large one) and a wonderful life and became partners in everything we did. Our relationship may not have been the most traditional, but we did not care, and we made it work. On Saturdays I may have been out in the yard doing yard work, landscaping, and gardening, and he was cleaning inside – not traditional roles – but he hated to be outside, and I love it, so that's what we did. I'm not saying everything was a bed of roses. Max had a lot to overcome due to the home life that he was raised in, but we worked through that and became a united team. We equally parented together – we have never lived in a home without a child. He adopted my child from my first marriage, and we had three more children and now two sons-in-law, a daughter-in-law, and four beautiful grandchildren (we now have another grandchild since his death). We did ministry together from church music ministry to hospitality/catering, etc. Whatever needed to be done we tried to do it. We were an amazing team – I'm not sure either of us individually would have been able to accomplish a fraction of what we were able to accomplish as a united team.

He cared so much about me (and everyone) and our wellbeing. I was left with nothing when I divorced and had no post-high school education or work experience. I married at eighteen the first time, and that was very concerning to Max, so, immediately after we were married, he told me, "Chris, you are very intelligent, and you need to go to college and get a degree and a career so that you will never be in a situation where you are not able to support yourself again if needed." Within a year or so of our marriage I went to nursing school and earned a BSN in nursing and have had an amazing career with an amazing company for the past nearly twenty-three years. I'm so grateful that he encouraged me to go to pursue a degree and did not worry that my degree and/or my career may have surpassed his: he just wanted the best for me and our family. He was my biggest supporter in everything I did. He cherished and treasured me and let the world know. He would often call me the "prettiest girl in the room" and even had a sign painted for me with these exact words for my birthday just a month or so before he was diagnosed with cancer. He loved his children deeply and hurt when they hurt and rejoiced when they rejoiced. He was a proud, loving Poppy, and he would have laid down his life for any of us. If someone needed something, he would assure that it was taken care of.

Back to the "secondhand store" comment: Max treasured and cherished me despite my wounds and scars – he showed me what true love and devotion were. God gave Max to me to build a life and family that is now part of me, and God took him away too young, too early, but God always has a plan. He did not have to give him to me in the first place. God did not owe me a second chance at knowing what a good marriage to a good, faithful man could be, but He did and took him away at a young age of sixty-one, so I cannot question Him. His ways are perfect, and He does all things well. He gives and He takes away – blessed be the name of the Lord. "The Lord gave, and the Lord hath taken away; blessed be the name of the Lord" ((Job 1:21) is engraved on his gravestone monument.)

Chapter 2

The First Month

January 16, 2023

I am five weeks into this grief process and have realized that nothing can prepare you for the process of grieving the loss of a spouse. Also, nothing can prevent you from going through the process. There is no way around it, no way to stop it – you must go through it. I have realized as well that there is no way for you to understand the pain of this process if you have not experienced it. You can imagine what it will be like, you can think through it the months you are by the side of your very ill spouse, you can hear others' stories about their process, but you cannot understand it until you are in the process. It is painful, it is difficult, it is overwhelming, and it is powerful. You can experience emotions that you never knew about or realized were possible. With that said, you can experience a closeness to God that you've never experienced. I have been through a lot of painful, grief-inducing experiences in life, and God has been very close with every situation, but He is especially close during this grieving process. I am so thankful that I have a covenant with Him and know that He is faithful in every circumstance if I stay faithful to Him. I will not be angry with Him. I will not pull myself away from Him.

I also have realized that there is really nothing that anyone can say to take the pain away, but I do know that the love and support from family, church family, coworkers, and friends is comforting. The texts, calls, Facebook messages, and cards lets me know that they all care and love me and have not forgotten the place where I am, and I appreciate the support so much. No matter what – God is still good, and He is faithful. "The LORD is close to the brokenhearted and saves those who are crushed in spirit" (Psalm 34:18 NIV).

Reflection

The "widow fog" is so real. I can barely remember writing these initial thoughts in the beginning of my grief process, so I am thankful that I did. This was written at a very raw phase of my grief process. The fog can be absolutely debilitating at times, causing the widow to be almost dysfunctional some days. I am not sure how, except by the grace of God, I got through these initial months with my demanding job. Also, by the date on this entry it was right at the time that my sump pump in my finished basement malfunctioned and my basement, where my engaged son lived, was flooded and required a complete remodel, which was a three-month process fighting with insurance, working with contractors, and waiting on construction supplies that were on back order. What an enormous amount of additional stress to a new widow.

I will mention cardinals a few times throughout this book, and I remember the day that the basement restoration was finally complete, and I went to close the garage door that had been open all day as the contractors were in and out of the house. I was in the opposite end of the house in my office working all day with all the commotion going on below me and at the other end of the house. I heard a frantic noise across the other side of the garage by one of the windows, so I went to see what was going on before I closed the door. That's when I found a beautiful cardinal frantically trying to get out of the closed window. The bird was working so hard and making no progress. I got a broomstick and moved the curtain and helped the cardinal turn around. It immediately saw the light at the garage door and flew away. I remember thinking my life felt just like that cardinal. I was working so hard and didn't feel like I was getting anything accomplished. I felt a nudge that said, "Chris, turn around and find a different way out of this darkness you are in." I felt it was a confirmation that God was right there and knew where I was, and He sent a cardinal that day to "show me a different way." I'm not saying that everything was easy and went smoothly from that day on, but the little comforting things that would happen along the way were always a reminder that I was not walking this journey alone.

Chapter 3

Sorrows Like Deep Billows Roll

February 4, 2023

I am eight weeks into this grief process and have realized some things about the journey. Journey is defined as moving from one place to the other. The journey of grief is moving from one phase to another. The opposite of journey may be defined as stagnation or immobility; so, I'm hoping that, even though I may move forward and then backwards again and then start the move forward again, that I am still journeying and will eventually get to the final phase of grief: "acceptance." I do know that everyone's journey is difficult, but it is different. I can't compare my journey to yours, and you should not compare yours to mine. When we go on a trip, we all choose to travel differently. We may all be headed to the same destination, but some may like to fly and get somewhere fast, some may like to drive and take the back roads and stop and sightsee along the way, or some may take a really slow trip on a train. Any way you choose to travel, hopefully, you will end up in the same place. This is the way I feel about the journey of grief. If I "travel" differently than you, that's okay – as long as I'm moving and not stagnant or immobile.

What about those sorrows like deep billows that roll

in many times without notice? I was walking through Kroger today and walked past the floral section and smelled all the fresh flowers and there came one of those billows because the smell reminded me of being surrounded by all the beautiful flowers at Max's viewing and funeral and then at my home for the days following the funeral. What about those Facebook memories? You feel like you're making progress and then a memory pops up that brings back the grief and how much you loved and now miss that person. What about driving down Hwy 31 and realize you're passing the cemetery and Max's and my dad's gravesites can be seen from the highway. I am told that these things become less and less sorrowful as time goes on, and I'm holding to that because this can be debilitating at times.

What I know is that God is still good, He is still faithful, and He is still close to the brokenhearted. He will walk with me on this journey of grief, and sometimes I know He is carrying me because I do not have the strength on my own. I can't tell you how many times I've felt as if I cannot make it, and someone reaches out to me at the right time with a word of encouragement or stops me at church to tell me that they are thinking of me and praying for me. Even if this makes me tear up and makes them feel uncomfortable, please don't hesitate to let me know because that's confirmation that God has not forgotten me, and He cares, and you care as well, and that means so much. If you are on a journey, keep moving, even if it's backwards at times. You cannot stay where you are. As long as you're moving, you're still alive, and when you're alive, there is always hope for better days.

Reflection

"It is Well" has always been one of my favorite songs. I have gleaned so much from it at different times of my life. It seems it can have a little different meaning as I travel through life and with different phases of life or different heartaches. Several years ago, I realized that there is a difference between "heart" and "soul." How can such heartache and sorrow be "well with my soul?" As I've matured and progressed through life, I now realize that, even when my heart is broken or even crushed by life circumstances or crushed by someone's actions, it may not be well with my "heart," but it is still well with my "soul," since my soul, as Merriam Webster would define it, is the "spiritual principle embodied in human beings." God has proven himself faithful throughout my life, and my soul is that part of me that puts my trust in Him and Him alone. My heart may break, but my soul knows it is well if I keep my covenant with Him. He will then keep His promises to me and get me through whatever comes my way.

> When peace like a river attendeth my way,
> When sorrows like sea billows roll;
> Whatever my lot Thou hast taught me to say,
> "It is well, it is well with my soul!"[1]
>
> ~Horatio Gates Spafford

Chapter 4

Painful "Happy Events"

There was a four-month period from February through June that I did not journal. These months were filled with big family events and other annual "firsts" and was a remarkably busy and stressful time. The demands of my job as I journeyed through this intensive grief process was beyond overwhelming. It was only by the grace of God that I was able to move through these months. I truly got a better understanding of the writings in Psalms during this time.

> Hear my cry, O God; attend unto my prayer. From the end of the earth will I cry unto thee, when my heart is overwhelmed: lead me to the rock that is higher than I. For thou hast been a shelter for me, and a strong tower from the enemy. I will abide in thy tabernacle for ever: I will trust in the covert of thy wings. Selah.
>
> Psalms 61:1 – 4

> He that dwelleth in the secret place of the most High shall abide under the shadow of the Almighty. I will say of the LORD, He is my refuge and my fortress: my God; in him will I trust. Surely he shall deliver thee from the snare of the fowler, and from

the noisome pestilence. He shall cover thee with his feathers, and under his wings shalt thou trust: his truth shall be thy shield and buckler. Thou shalt not be afraid for the terror by night; nor for the arrow that flieth by day; Nor for the pestilence that walketh in darkness; nor for the destruction that wasteth at noonday. A thousand shall fall at thy side, and ten thousand at thy right hand; but it shall not come nigh thee. Only with thine eyes shalt thou behold and see the reward of the wicked. Because thou hast made the LORD, which is my refuge, even the most High, thy habitation; There shall no evil befall thee, neither shall any plague come nigh thy dwelling. For he shall give his angels charge over thee, to keep thee in all thy ways.

Psalms 91:1 – 11

At the time of Max's terminal diagnosis, I began feeling the presence of angels, and they comforted me through that last month of his life, at the time of his death, and during those first initial months. This was not a common occurrence for me prior to this life event and think it was a little concerning for the few family members that I would speak to about this. I will say a little more about this in the last chapter. I believe that God knew these were unbearable times for me, and He sent a little extra, personal comfort (angels to keep charge over me) to help me navigate my way and hold me up during these extremely dark days.

In March I traveled to Florida for my nephew's wedding. This was a long road trip from my home in Indiana, and I needed to attend and assure my mother got there as well. This was the first big event without my dad and Max, and it was a very difficult painful time. My brother had also just been diagnosed with liver cancer the previous month and was not able to attend due to being in chemotherapy treatment. It seemed our large family was rapidly melting away. Navigating a long road trip and attending a social event was so difficult – I was so lost without Max by my side. I missed his sense of humor, his stability, and his strength. I was so sad and felt that I was a "downer" to a happy event, but it was a painful happy event for me.

A short four weeks later I had to do it all over again. It was my son's wedding in Northern Indiana, so I had to attend! This was a wonderful event and Chris had found a beautiful young lady, and Max and I were so thankful for God's blessing and restoration in Chris' life. However, this was just four months after Max's death, and I was still in a "widow fog" and some days barely able to get out of bed due to the overwhelming grief. I had also just, finally, gotten the basement flood restoration project completed after three months and was trying to keep up with things at work. When our daughters had gotten married, Max and I both loved weddings and enjoyed the events to the fullest, but he was not here for this one – a day we had prayed about for several years. My sister-in-law, Leah, came up from Tennessee to help me through that event and lightened my load, and I'm thankful for her.

In May and June, summer was approaching. I had yard work and gardening to keep up with and a summer cabin at our Indiana district church campground to de-winterize and open for the camp season – something that Max always took care of. We were also awarded a new "start-up" site at work, and I had to travel to Idaho for a couple of weeks in May. Although I had traveled for work for years, travel since Max's death has been very difficult both emotionally and physically. Before Max's death, he took on full responsibility of our home while I was gone, and I never had to worry, but now I would become anxious and worried about my home while I was gone. It was also exhausting to be away from home. The grieving process is very exhausting and wondering whether I could hold up physically was a concern and caused episodes of anxiety that I was not accustomed to. Times were tough and I pushed through. God, my children, and a few close friends got me through that rough season.

Another thing that got me through these rough months, and still does, is my love for music. As mentioned, prayer and Bible reading, as well as reading through devotionals that I have been gifted has been a necessity through this process. However, there are times that you just don't have the strength to read or pray – I'm just being honest. I listen to music a lot during the day, but on those nights when grief would overtake me and I could not even sleep, God would give me a song in the night, or I would play music softly as I'd try to sleep. There are so many times that just the right song would play that would minister to me. I entered this in a journal just recently on Tuesday, November 21, 2023.

I was mopping the dining room trying to prepare for Thanksgiving – first since Max' death. The song "Jireh" (Elevation Music and Maverick City Music)[2] came on. This song ministered to me last year during Max's final illness. I became overwhelmed due to pain I was having from a fall a few days before. I began weeping and telling God – yes, You are enough, but I'm not enough. The song ended and Lauren Daigle's "You Say" began playing, which says, "I keep fighting voices in my mind that say I'm not enough." The song then goes on to say, "You say I am loved when I can't feel a thing. You say I am strong when I think I am weak." This was definitely a God moment! I then looked down at the verse at the bottom of the journal I was writing in. "Be strong and courageous! For the Lord your God is with you wherever you go" (Joshua 1:9, NIV).

Chapter 5

Reality – The Six-Month Mark

June 23, 2023

Grief is exhausting, unpredictable, confusing, excruciating, overwhelming, and sometimes filled with a darkness – a darkness that is sometimes comforting. How can you explain that? It brings feelings, responses, and behaviors out of you that you never knew you were capable of. It is different for every loss you may experience and different for every person, even if it seems as if your loss was similar. It is comparable to none. It cannot be avoided, it cannot be explained, it cannot be shortened, and sometimes, it feels it cannot be overcome but will overcome you.

You feel a need to be around people and then realize that need is too much, and you must draw yourself back and deal with things in a dark, private place. I've found that's okay, and God will meet you there. He is not far away from the brokenhearted. In fact, He is very close.

Being a "younger widow" is more difficult than I had ever imagined. I've had many people tell me, "At least you're still working and have something to occupy your mind." On some days, this may be true, since I do have a demanding career, but on other days it's overwhelming and often hard to function.

It may even delay the grieving process since you cannot take the time needed to work through things mentally and emotionally but must stay driven to perform professionally at the level your job requires. The other thing I did not take into consideration was the duties at home that multiply when you lose a spouse, especially when your spouse equally shared household duties. This can make home and work life extremely overwhelming.

I am so thankful for my kids and family that are so patient and accommodating. I can't imagine life without them, but I know they are grieving too, and I find it difficult to not be the "strong mom" they are used to. It's painful to also see them grieve. I am also thankful for my friends and those that are comfortable with being around me and are not turned away by my tears. I am so thankful for individuals that share my grief – this is a special talent and ministry and these individuals I know God has put into my life for "such a time as this." Some may not even realize what a blessing they've been to me.

I know things will change. They will get better and, as my pastor recently told me, "It will not always be this painful" but, until then, I will keep moving through this process at my own pace. Thanks for being patient with me....

Reflection:

By the end of July, I was so overwhelmed with responsibilities of life and work that I decided I would have to take a respite, time off from work, to be able to successfully continue on this grief journey. I had to work through some things and get some order to my "new normal." I had been working with a grief counselor through my EAP at work and she had suggested a respite, so, after much thought, I decided to take a sixty-day leave. This was a wonderful time of solace. Indiana was blessed during this time with some beautiful weather, and I spent my days outside working in my yard and flower garden. I have always loved to garden and find that it brings me closer to God and nature and is restorative for me. I had to come to grips with and accept the reality of my new normal and find a way to thrive or at least survive until the time that I could thrive. I was so hesitant the first seven months of my grief process to do this since I knew I was needed at work. This has also been something new for me – being able to put myself and my needs first, but thankfully I came to the realization that it was a necessity, and I am so thankful I decided to take the leave of absence. The day before I was returning to work after sixty days, I found out my brother had days to weeks to live. That was September 25th, and he passed away on October 15th.

Chapter 6

The Chair – To Sit or Not to Sit?

July 16, 2023

Grief causes you to think about things that you never had given much thought to before. I had heard people in the past – prior to my own experience – say things such as, "no one has sat in his chair since he has been gone" or "we feel it's disrespectful to sit in her chair" or "no one can fill his shoes (or chair)." None of this was of much importance to me until I began walking (crawling) this grief journey.

In one of the last visits when our family was all together near to the time of Max's death, we were all gathered around the large dining room table. Max was too sick to make it to the table to sit with us in his normal chair at the head of the table. Everyone was hesitant as to whether they should sit in "his chair" although it was likely he was no longer going to be sitting there. Max realized the awkwardness of it all, so he assigned the seat to his only son by birth, Christopher, so that's where he sits now when we're all gathered. He was always thinking of others and even in his last days did not want us to leave a seat empty at the table, feeling we would, in some way, be disrespecting him. He knew that really wouldn't make much sense as our family is growing, and we needed the seat for gathering, so he was thoughtful enough to "assign" it prior to his leaving us.

Max had another "special lawn chair" (if you know, you know☺) that I had bought him, and he took it with him to men's retreat, T-ball games, cookouts, picnics, fireworks display, etc. I sometimes put this chair in the driveway from the garage and sit in it for a while. I took it today to Leo's birthday party, since it was outside. He had a recliner (right side of our reclining love seat) that was "his seat" when we gathered in the living area and any time he was in the living room. He spent a lot of time in this chair since 2020, the year he was down with a back injury and then surgery in June of that year. He even had to sleep in this chair for months. He then spent a lot of time in that chair in 2022 during his terminal illness, chemo, post-surgery, and end of life. In most pictures you'd see him in our home, he was normally in this chair. I sometimes sit in this seat and look at "his world" that he viewed for weeks and months at times. Our children and their spouses sometimes sit in this seat when they come to visit me.

Now back to the question, to sit or not to sit? I am not sure where society came up with the unwritten rules that come after a death of someone, but for me, sit in the seat if it brings you comfort as it does me when I sit for a while in his recliner. I do not feel at all that I'm being disrespectful, and I know that he would expect us to use that seat. He would probably be very surprised how many times, and the amount of time, I have sat in his recliner since sitting in the living room has never been a common occurrence throughout our nearly thirty-four-year marriage, and

I bet he would be happy for me if he knew that I did sit in his chair occasionally.

I've said all this to say – there are no rules in grieving. Everyone has their own journey, and if it brings you sadness, don't sit in their chair. If it brings you comfort, sit in it. This is your own personal journey and do whatever you find helpful or comforting. For me, I will sit in the seat and enjoy seeing my kids sit there as well. It brings me comfort and reminds me of him. How can that be "against the rules?"

Reflection:

I want to talk about the "individualized grieving process." Being there are three new widows in our family within eighteen months, it is very evident that we all grieve differently. No one can tell someone how to grieve or to not grieve. This is a very personal journey. Although I've had some very insensitive things said to me throughout this journey, I cannot fault folks for things they say "out of ignorance." When I say, "out of ignorance," I am not trying to be hateful or judgmental, but it is so true that you cannot understand this if you have not traveled this journey yourself. I'm thankful if you have not experienced it. You can be educated on the subject, but it's hard to know the full impact without the experience. You cannot feel that others should have the same experience as you if you have traveled your own journey. Every loss is different depending on the relationship between the individuals.

Grief is a very long journey,
a journey you take on your own.
And no one can know
all the sorrow you feel,
for it is your sorrow alone.
Grief is an awful intruder,
it comes and it stays
night and day.
And no one can look
at the way that you grieve,
and then tell you,
"No, this is the way."[3]

~Anne Peterson

Shortly after the funeral my daughters and I were talking and I said, "I think we should write a book on 'what not to say at the casket.'" As I am a year out I think the shorter book would be "what to say at the casket." Sometimes saying nothing is the best solution if you are uncomfortable or awkward about the situation. I have found the most helpful things that people have said to me are:

- I am so sorry.
- I just don't understand.
- I am praying for you.
- I am praying for you and your family.
- You're in my thoughts and prayers.
- He was a great man.
- I know this is a huge loss.
- We loved him too.

Other things that are helpful are those individuals that keep sending cards, texts, other messages of encouragement, or just say "I'm thinking about you" or "I'm praying for you today." I have so many cards that I have saved that I have received since Dad and Max's death. Some that I received at the very beginning of this journey I hardly remember, but I will sit and pull a few out in a time of sorrow or deep discouragement and read them to remind myself of how much I'm loved and cared about. The other thing that is so encouraging and comforting is when others still talk about Max. Max was a friend to everyone and had a one-on-one ministry of encouragement. I have had people tell me stories of encouraging things that he did that I never knew about. He also had such a sense of humor and was so funny. I love to hear those funny stories as well. One of the things that first attracted me to him was his sense of humor and intelligence. He was so much fun. We laughed a lot throughout our year of dating and our nearly thirty-four years of marriage.

Chapter 7

Your Grieving Children and Grandchildren

August 14, 2023

One of the things that is the most difficult on this journey is seeing your children and grandchildren grieve the loss. The thought of them not having their father/Poppy in their lives is heartbreaking for me as a mother, and I cannot do anything about it.

Friday, when Leo and I were at the zoo, he kept asking me questions about Poppy and where he is now, and it made me realize that, as hard as it is for me to wrap my heart and mind around the reality that Max is no longer here with us, I can't imagine how difficult it is for a three-year-old child. How do you answer Lyndon's question – soon after Max's death – about whether Poppy has his phone in heaven? Poppy would often FaceTime our grandbabies, and I'm sure that's what Lyndon was hoping to do. ☺

Christopher always teased us about being the "old parents" but never realized he would lose his father at twenty-four years old, and our daughter-in-law barely got to know him. Adrian is having our first grandchild since our loss, and this baby will never know Poppy. I'm sure it feels so different at our home for all our children, and I feel so sorry about that. They had one of the best dads who loved his children and grands deeply. They were his pride and joy. He loved the home and family we had built and would do anything for any of them.

I know my children are strong, and they will be alright – the process is just difficult. We can only keep memories alive and make new ones – that's what Max would expect us to do.

Reflection:

Often, when families go through so much tragedy, they fall away from God or drift apart from each other. I am thankful to say that, over the past year, I believe we have all grown closer to God and to each other. We are moving past the initial shock and the obvious-gaping absence of Max in our lives, still keeping his memory alive, and creating new memories. He loved life and family and would be so sad to know how difficult this has been for all of us. One of our daughters, Adrian, began a hashtag on social media at the time we knew he was terminal (#MyDadMax), and we still post memories of him or updates to our lives. I also memorialized his Facebook page so that we or others can go to his page and post things about him.

Navigating this complex grief process as a widow as well as trying to support my children and grandchildren in their grief has been very challenging. I think my adult children have always seen me as a strong person and seeming so weak and vulnerable is difficult for me. I think the thing that has been helpful is that I have given myself permission to grieve, even if that is openly. What I have found is that my adult children have been very supportive and gives them permission to grieve as well. They are strong and resilient, and, as time goes on, we are becoming even stronger and compassionate because of our own heartbreaks and challenges. We are striving to continue Max's legacy and make new memories of our own.

Our grandchildren are very young (the oldest grandsons were five and six years old at the time they lost their "Poppy", and the two younger ones were three and nearly three). Seeing them grieve and trying to wrap their little minds and hearts around it has been agonizing, especially the older ones who have more memories and realize that death is final. They watched their great grandfather in his illness and then in his casket just eight months prior to their Poppy. Then ten months after seeing their Poppy they saw their young, great uncle. Trying to explain to young children that someone is "very sick" and then soon after explaining why they are "gone" was very difficult for their parents. We must now be careful about telling them someone is "sick" because they immediately think that the result is going to be death. As a grandmother, I continue to love and support my grandchildren and pray for their young minds and hearts. I also welcome any conversations or questions that they may bring up with me and let them know I'm comfortable with talking about their Poppy. I do believe that these early life experiences can result in compassionate, empathetic adults in later years, so I pray for that outcome and not an outcome of bitterness and distrust and lack of faith in a faithful God.

For this Christmas (2023) I made all the grandchildren a small teddy bear out of one of his shirts. I had an idea to use shirts in which I had a picture of Poppy with a specific grandchild. I then gave the child a 5X7 printed, framed picture with the teddy bear so that they would know it really was Poppy's shirt because they had a picture of him and them when he was wearing it. Below is my daughter Emily's Facebook post on Christmas evening.

> "Christmas with my family was quite different this year. However, we had such a great day with family, and it reminds me of how blessed we are!
>
> My mom made teddy bears out of some of my dad's shirts for the grandkids. To top it all off, she framed a picture of my dad when he wore the shirt so they could always remember him. Such a special gift! When we came home Lyndon said "my favorite gift today was the poppy teddy bear." ☺ ☺
>
> Thank you, Mom, and Rachel for such a thoughtful gift." ♥♥♥

Chapter 8

Keep Moving

September 21, 2023

My mother recently said to me, "I did something the other day I thought I'd never do." She went on to tell me she went to Dad's gravesite and talked to him. Grief will cause you to do things that you never thought you would do or cause you to do things you may have questioned that others did in their grief. I have found this to be true for myself. I have always been a strong, keep-pushing-through-the-pain, comeback type of personality despite the struggles, challenges, and heartaches I've had in life, but this grief journey has knocked me down for the count. You often do things to try to soften the blow or deal with the intense emotional (and sometimes physical) pain. Sometimes it helps, sometimes it does not.

One other thing that I have recognized is that I may feel that I should avoid a certain memory or activity, afraid of bringing more emotional pain or anguish, but as I force myself to do it, it becomes therapeutic. This may be cleaning out Max's belongings or, as I did recently, pull out all his fall décor and decorate the house. It was surprisingly therapeutic. I do want to caution, that, even though something may or may not have been therapeutic for you, do not think it is the same for me or for others. We must all travel this journey for ourselves without others' comparisons. No loss is the same, even if it may seem the same. Just as relationships are different, losses are equally different. Other things that you do not realize may cause so much pain do cause intense pain, such as attending our UPCI General Conference this week for the first time without Max. It has been excruciating and even physically painful, but I cannot "ignore life" for the rest of mine, so I push through, hoping it gets better with time. I have those who have told me I am so strong, but I feel so weak. I am thankful for the strength of God, my ever-present help and comforter. Don't get me wrong, and please don't judge me, but I do wonder why life must be so hard and painful at times, but I cannot question. I know He has a plan and a purpose for my life, just as He always has. I just must keep the faith and keep moving forward. As my dad used to say, "if you're not moving forward, you're going backwards," so I must keep moving forward even if it's at a snail's pace.

Reflection:

This is one of the most difficult parts of this journey – to keep moving. Not only do you need to keep moving but ensure your moves are positive. As I have traveled this journey, especially at the start of the journey, I can understand why some individuals resort to not so positive measures to get through the initial pain of their situation. Some may resort to alcohol or drugs, but this will complicate your situation and even delay the grief process. If you cannot find coping mechanisms such as I have mentioned in this book or through a counselor or a support group such as GriefShare, or if you are struggling and cannot move forward, and your coping mechanisms and/or support system or group is not helping, and you feel hopeless, please seek medical care. (A local GriefShare group can be found at Find a Group - GriefShare.org)

I have heard a lot about the difference between "moving forward" and "moving on." Please know that moving forward does not mean that you have forgotten your loved one or that it is disrespectful to them. I cannot imagine Max wanting me to stay in misery and in a dark place for the rest of my life. He expects me and our family to move forward. Of course, we will keep his memory alive, but we must be realistic in the fact that nothing is going to bring him back, and we must make the best of our new situation, our new normal.

Chapter 9

Making Progress on Your Journey

November 22, 2023

I avoided going into Hobby Lobby for over a year. Max loved that store, and it was the last place we shopped together. On November 5, 2022, we went into Hobby Lobby and Max seemed to be on a mission buying new fall décor as well as some new Christmas decorations to change up our Christmas trees. I snapped a couple of pictures as he filled his cart and shopped as if it was going to be his last Christmas. This was prior to having a scan the following week that showed he had terminal liver cancer, but I think, in his heart, he knew that would be his last "shopping spree." We received his scan results on the following Saturday, and he became very ill that next week. He was never able to decorate for Christmas last year. I decorated as he watched from his chair when he came home from the hospital on hospice on November 29th. He assured me everything looked great although that is probably not the exact plans he had for the new decorations.

Grief and response to events can change as you move through the process. What may have been unbearable months ago was tolerable when I finally went into

Hobby Lobby last week, more than a year past the last time I was in there with Max. After his death, and for months, I would get an overwhelming feeling and what felt like nausea every time I passed the store, but I was finally able to overcome that feeling and go into the store and buy a few more decorations for the tree this year that would add a little bit of "Chris flair" to it. I think he would love that!

Although this is the first Thanksgiving since Max's death, he was in the hospital over Thanksgiving last year. We were able to FaceTime so that he could talk to everyone, but he was not there, and we had Thanksgiving dinner at Mom's house instead of ours. This year I am doing Thanksgiving at my house for the first time without him and his help. All of it is overwhelming, more emotionally than physically, but I'm doing it and I think he would also be pleased with it all. He was always my biggest help and my biggest supporter, and he is so missed. I know the holidays are so difficult for all our family and trying to keep as much normalcy as possible is my goal no matter how difficult it is.

Next up is Christmas – in reality, it's our second Christmas without Max since he passed away on December 11th last year, but since I don't remember anything about last Christmas, it will be the first without him for me. He loved the holidays, and knowing he isn't here to celebrate with his family makes my heart hurt for him; although, I know that's ridiculous since he's resting peacefully and doesn't even miss us! ☺ Sometimes I'm envious of that, but I sure want to be around for my kids!

I guess what I'm saying is moving through the process is progress. I would not want to be stuck in the same stage or phase of grief forever. Could I avoid Hobby Lobby forever? Probably, but I'm not sure it's really the best way (for me) to deal with grief!

Reflection:

At the time of Max's death, being it was at Christmas time, I had a couple of people give me tree ornaments with pictures of him on them. I decided I would put up a Max's memorial tree this year. Max loved Christmas and had a lot of Christmas neckties that he had collected over the years. I had decided I would make a tree skirt out of them and use the picture ornaments but had not decided for sure what else I would decorate the seven-foot tree with. On a second trip to Hobby Lobby, I wandered down an aisle and came across nearly a whole aisle of cardinals. I had become fascinated with cardinals since my dad and Max's death, and it was perfect. I also added cardinals to a wreath that Max had made a few years ago and to my fireplace mantel. I found beautiful throw pillows for "his chair" (the loveseat), and my daughter, Rachel, bought me a beautiful snow globe with cardinals in it that sits on the end table by his chair and the tree. It was perfect! I then received five other cardinal ornaments from friends and coworkers this Christmas. This tree will be an annual tradition. Our new grandbaby, a beautiful healthy girl, arrived on December 22, 2023 – such a blessing. Adrian and Kyle had a miscarriage right at the time that Max was terminal in 2022, so this was a reminder of God's promises and restoration.

I posted this on Facebook on December 15, 2023, to sum up the year since Max's homegoing funeral service.

Tomorrow will be one year that we laid Max to rest. As I look back over the year, it's been by the grace of God that I've had the emotional and physical strength to get through all the events of the year.

In January my basement flooded, and it was a three-month project getting it livable again. I had to do things that Max would have normally done such as dealing with insurance and contractors.

We had two big family weddings this year with one being our son's. It was very difficult without Max there to celebrate the happy event. The loneliness at those type of events is something that no one can fix. We were always partners in everything we did, and the vacancy was loud and clear. He would have been so happy if he was there. We then, unfortunately, had another family funeral that I had to face without his support.

I've had to take my car for oil changes and have things such as have brakes replaced and filters changed. Not that I can't do it but knowing he always did it makes his absence very obvious. I've also learned to fix things and do minor maintenance at my house, and I've had kind people to help when I needed it. Rachel has also been a big help, and you should see us sometimes figuring things out and fixing things. We've relied on YouTube or just got it done by trial and error. ☺

I went to camp (including opening and then having the cabin winterized) and conferences without him. It's difficult, but I'm a young widow and can't just sit at home for whatever time I have to live. I have learned to "push through" as I've often honestly told folks that ask how I'm doing. Pushing through is necessary if I want to "move forward." As I've quoted my dad before, "if you're not moving forward, you'll go backwards." I definitely don't want to do that. Whatever that would mean in my situation I'm not sure, but it doesn't sound like it'd be a positive thing!

As I move into the Holidays and into a new year, both on the calendar, and in my phase of life, I'm not sure what tomorrow brings, but I know Who holds tomorrow. I'm so grateful for those who have prayed for and with me and supported me this past year. I feel so blessed with those that have surrounded me with an outpouring of love and support. I have had new opportunities at church that have given me purpose, and I'm so grateful for that. Also, I'm so thankful for my family: I have the most amazing kids. They have been through so much but have also persevered and kept on with life like champs. Now we await our new bundle of joy, Caroline June - we look forward to celebrating new life. ♥
#MyDadMax

Chapter 10

Choices

December 31, 2023

I was working on a puzzle this past week and found it to be much more difficult than I thought it would be by the picture on the box. As I continued to work and contemplate why it seemed so difficult – it was a seemingly simple puzzle, the picture did not seem complicated, and it was only 500 pieces – it dawned on me that it was the shape of the pieces. They were not the normal, simple shapes of puzzles I had completed in the past. Many places where it seemed one piece should have been, it was split into two strangely shaped pieces. In other places it seemed as if it should have been two pieces, but I would come across a very odd-shaped piece that would fit in there perfectly. I was then aware that I would have to change the way I looked at the puzzle and change the way I would choose my pieces if I wanted to be successful in completing it.

As a new year is approaching, I was reflecting on the past year since Max's death as I worked on the puzzle. I began to think of how my life had changed so drastically, and how I, too, had to look at things much differently as I moved through the grief process and found my way the past year without my husband of nearly thirty-four years, my biggest supporter and advocate. I had to make choices on my own that Max and I would normally have made together. I had to make choices based on a new normal that, quite honestly, I did not ask for, did not think was "fair," and did not want to have to adjust to. Just as completing the puzzle, if I wanted to successfully finish my life, whatever time God allows me to have, I had to change the way I looked at things and make choices that were best for me and help me to move forward successfully.

2024 is here tomorrow and I must make choices that will help me to move to the next phase of grief and life. I must make hard choices at times regarding how I spend my time, who I surround myself with, and coping mechanisms I adopt. I must advocate for myself since Max is no longer here to advocate for me. I must make thoughtful and prayerful choices that will help me successfully navigate being a widow (a title I really dislike and have avoided calling myself, but it's the harsh reality, and I must accept it in order to move forward). Many times, decisions I make may not seem to make sense to others or be what they think is best for me, but this is my journey and the path that God has chosen for me, so I will embrace it and travel the journey prayerfully, hopefully with humbleness and grace with God's help. I will surround myself with people who are positive and have supported me the past year and others that God may put in my path going forward that will walk alongside me and lovingly support me when I feel the journey is too long or too rough to complete. Of course, God will be right there and carry me when needed just as He has done this past year. He knows the way that I take and has plans for me. I put all my trust in Him and in Him only. "For I know the plans I have for you, declares the Lord, plans to prosper you and not to harm you, plans to give you hope and a future" (Jeremiah 29:11 NIV).

Happy New Year to you all. Much love to those that have gotten me through 2023 – the roughest year of my life....

Reflection:

I am aware that my grief journey is not over. I am aware that those waves and billows of sorrow will sweep over me from time to time, but I am hopeful that things will progressively get better. I am sure that life and family events as well as random trivial things will bring the waves in, but I must find a way to ride the waves. I am also aware that God is in control and that He knows my beginning and the ending. I have heard all my life about my birth and how the umbilical cord was extremely long and wrapped around my neck multiple times and how my mother prayed that I would live. I grew up in a very sheltered environment and had an uneventful childhood, but my adult life has been filled with joy and sorrow, much more than I could have been able to comprehend as a young, sheltered girl. I have often said, I am so thankful that God does not allow us to see our future. I would not have been able to bear it, but I am who I am today, a better person, because of tribulation and overcoming by faithfulness to God and His help.

Thoughts On Grief—My Journey Through The Grief Process

I heard a song several months into my grief process that I could have written – the words were so applicable to my life: "Never Walk Alone" ~Hope Darst[4]

God is so faithful, and I'll never walk alone.

Chapter 11

Sweet Remembrance of Those Last Days

December 10, 2023

The one-year anniversary of Max's passing is tomorrow December 11th. I must admit I do not remember much after his funeral, but it's been an emotional week as each date reminds me of what was happening on that specific date last year. It's quite perplexing that these details are so embedded in my brain. I'm sure the details will fade some as years pass, but right now, it is very fresh in my mind.

Max had come home from the hospital on home hospice on November 29th. There was a lot of activity as home care staff, home care equipment suppliers, and friends were coming to visit. On November 30th, it was a Wednesday evening and Rachel and I were decorating Christmas trees for Max to enjoy and watching our midweek service online and Max had a bad fall which was very frightening for him. Our wonderful neighbor came over to assist with getting him up and reality hit – this process is going very rapidly. We continued through the days with visitors in and out as I was caring for a very ill and declining Max.

Thoughts On Grief—My Journey Through The Grief Process

On Monday, December 5th, our kids, and funeral director had been here, and we had made final funeral arrangements, and again, a lot of activity and folks were in and out. Later in the afternoon, when it was quiet, Max asked me to sit down for a while, and he began asking me if I thought he'd be here on Christmas. The medical side of me knew that, without a divine miracle, it probably was unlikely as quickly as he was declining, and he had not eaten for weeks, so I told him honestly, as our communication had always been, that I could not see how that was possible unless God reached down and healed him, as we both knew He could. He calmly and peacefully told me, "Thanks for being so honest. I am going to start my journey home now," which he did.

Max had made a very adamant decision when agreeing to come home on hospice that he did not want to pass in our home. He did not want our children to have that memory in their family home. The hospice staff knew that and were prepared for him to be transferred to the facility when it was obvious that the time was nearing. He began "transitioning" on Wednesday the 7th, but there were no beds open at the facility. That evening, we remember the last lucid conversations we had with him and then it became obvious he was not "totally with us at all times." We sat up all night with him in the living room and what a beautiful spiritual time it was as he was transitioning with part of him still "here" and his obvious visions of heaven, talking with God, and occasionally still cognizant enough to say some things to us. I have very sweet memories of that night as I sat on the other side of his recliner in our loveseat throughout the night and knew he was getting ready to meet his Savior.

The next morning on December 8th, we were notified that a bed had opened at the facility, and they were setting up transport to come and transport him. We were scurrying around getting ready with the hospice nurses and you could tell he was getting very confused, but in his cognizant moments, happy to be going to the facility.

During the ride and upon arrival to the facility, he became extremely confused and very upset that "they did not let his wife come with him." Once I was able to see him in his room and I assured him it was me, he was satisfied. They medicated him and assured me he was comfortable, and he closed his eyes prepared to finish his "journey home." We then waited... for nearly three days – the most agonizing part of it all. Early on Sunday morning December 11th, around 4:53 a.m., he completed his journey home. Emily and I were both sound asleep at opposite ends of the bed when we both rose up at the exact same time as he took his last breath... I believe an angel may have brushed through the room waking us both up. His journey was over – he went home. It was agonizing but a beautiful experience. Two different individuals that did not know each other (one from work and one from church) had a dream very close to that time, of Max coming by to tell them goodbye, which is so something that Max would have liked to do. He was so social and a great friend and responsible employee. The vacancy and loss that we feel is still very painful, but by God's mercy and grace, we are progressing and moving through the grief process.

We are now focused on life, instead of death, as we anxiously await the arrival of little Caroline June. God has been good to us….

Reflection:

I am so thankful for the spiritual homegoing that Max experienced, and we were able to experience alongside of him. Watching two strong men (my dad and husband) deteriorate in front of us, eaten up with cancer, within an eight-month period, is not something that anyone would choose to do, but I'm thankful it was a beautiful peaceful ending. I am also thankful that we have a hope, and we know that heaven is a beautiful, carefree, pain free, glorious place. Who would not want that for your loved one. However, the reality is that we are still here in this troublesome place and must now find our way without the patriarch of our family, our biggest supporter and advocate. I do see his strengths in our children and am thankful for that. They have been a tremendous support to me and to each other. They are remarkable humans!

Chapter 12

Whatever Thy Hands Find to Do

I authored the article below several years ago for the UPCI Ladies Ministry and now find myself in a similar situation.

> As I was serving at our Indiana District's Women of Worth Tea, the speaker was talking to the widows of licensed ministers, and my mind went back many years to my personal situation. At the youthful age of eighteen I became a minister's wife, a full-time evangelist's wife at age twenty, and just as quickly as I became a minister's wife, I was not.
>
> After nearly two years of being on the road in a thirty-two-foot travel trailer, preaching revivals throughout the state, it all came to a stop on a late summer day at the Indiana District UPCI Campground. An all-day meeting was held which resulted in the revoking of my then husband's ministerial license. It was quite a scandal, and I was no longer a minister's wife – actually, within months I was not a wife at all, but a single mother, with a two-year-old child with disabilities.

As I listened to the speaker encouraging the widows to find whatever they could find to do, I remembered that being exactly what I made a decision to do in 1986 when my world was turned upside down, dreams crushed, trust broken, and heart broken. I could make a decision to become bitter, blame God for my situation, or find whatever I could find to do for the Kingdom.

My father was a church planter, and I began serving in his church playing music and leading worship. I served in any way that I could find to serve, in addition to music, whether it was baking cookies for bake sales, teaching Sunday school, picking people up for church, etc. (There was always something to do in Home Missions!)

Several years later I met a young man who asked me to be his wife and he adopted my daughter who was five years old at the time we married. We have served together in any way we saw a need for thirty years now. He has never had a ministerial license, but we have found that "ministering" does not require a license. We have served in music ministry, special events such as banquets and Sunday school contests, janitorial services, Bible studies, new convert discipleship, etc.

My life may have not followed the path I thought it was going to, but I am a witness of the faithfulness of God when we are faithful to Him even when heartbreak blindsides us in this thing called life. "Whatsoever thy hand findeth to do, do it with thy might..." (Ecclesiastes 9:10).

These events happened when I was a young twenty-two-year-old divorcee, and now I find myself a fifty-nine-year-old (now sixty) widow. So, I have followed the same path I did as a twenty-two year old divorcee during this season of my life: I find things to do, to find purpose and minister in any way that I can find to do. I serve in the music department at Calvary Tabernacle in Indianapolis in the choir and on the praise/worship team, I play keyboard about once a month at our Spanish service and have begun to help with music at another of our new smaller campuses. I cater meals for church events and assist with the GriefShare group. Anything that I can find to do, I want to do it to the best of my ability and serve with purpose.

Chapter 13

Caregiver Role Strain

In nursing school, we had to learn about "nursing diagnoses." These are different than a diagnosis given by a physician and are identified and given by nurses. A nursing diagnosis is defined by NANDA International (2013) as "a clinical judgment concerning a human response to health conditions/life processes, or vulnerability for that response, by an individual, family, group, or community." I do not hear much about these nursing diagnoses in recent years, but during our clinical rotations decades ago, we had to identify a nursing diagnosis for the patient(s) we were caring for that day and write a "Nursing Care Plan" for that specific patient and/or family. For some reason, of all the 235 or so NANDA nursing diagnoses, Caregiver Role Strain is the one that became embedded in my brain. I remember, in my early nursing career, working Neonatal Intensive Care and pediatrics where there were babies and children needing extensive medical care and often required this care at home or required parents to stay by their children's bedside during long and/or frequent hospitalizations. When I was an administrator of a home care agency, family members had their spouses, child, or parents needing full-time care at home to avoid placing them in long-term care facilities, and I would discuss care giver role strain with them and encourage them to take care of themselves or they would not be able to take care of their loved ones. Then, later in life, I had to practice this.

My mother was Dad's primary care giver, and I assisted her, especially after his surgery when he required IV fluids and injections, and at the end of his life. As mentioned previously, this was a two-year process and his last four months I was also caring for my husband while he was in rigorous chemotherapy treatments. A month after my dad's passing was Max's complex, radical surgery that required a long hospitalization and extensive care when he first arrived home including continuous tube feedings and other care and assistance. He never fully got back to his former, full functioning and required some assistance or required me to begin taking on more duties at home for him to continue working his job through his fatigue, etc. Then, just several months later, he was diagnosed with terminal cancer and there was a month of complete care up to the time that he went to a hospice facility the last few days.

I played the caregiver role and at the same time continued to work my demanding job and handled it all with consistency and without missing a beat. My mother had a serious fall about eight months after Max passed away and had to be transferred to a trauma center which was the same place that I had spent time with Max at the end of his life. I knew that the wait in the emergency room (ER) until he was assigned an inpatient bed was about twenty hours each time. This hospital was not accommodating to individuals accompanying patients, and I had sat those twenty hours with Max in straight back chairs without any sleep, and it caused a reaction in me that could have been described like a post-traumatic stress disorder episode. Everything that was going on was exaggerated for me, and I had to care for my mother while working through this emotional process that seemed to overtake me right in the middle of my initial grief process. Mom was in the hospital for a couple of days and then required care when she was discharged home. When she returned in a couple of weeks or so for a follow up scan of the internal bleed she had from the fall, a malignant tumor was discovered on her kidney, and she then had to have surgery and required care again. All my siblings live out of state, so I am grateful for my adult daughter, Rachel, that lives with me and helped to care for her. My sister-in-law, Leah, also came up from Tennessee to stay with her for several days. Less than two months later, Mom fell and broke her right (dominant) hand in two places. I mention all of this to say how, in previous years, or before the death of my husband, I would have taken these things in stride but having this type of stress on top of trying to keep your grieving self from crumbling was a challenging task. God has been faithful and carried me through it all. I know I could not have found the strength on my own. His strength is perfect when my strength is gone.

Chapter 14

Summary of Thoughts
Still Everything

When Max and I were planning his homegoing (funeral) service, there was one song that we wanted sung. It had been recorded by Indiana Bible College (IBC) at the beginning of the year. It summed up our feelings and would be a testament to our faith in God throughout our lives but especially throughout his illness. Max often talked to visitors — that would come by to visit in the hospital and at home during his last days — about the goodness of God and his (our) situation not changing, that God was still God, and He was still good. Max and I, along with our children, had sung "Goodness of God" at my dad's funeral just eight months before, and we still believed that. We had a peace that passed all understanding (Philippians 4:7), and because of prayers we had prayed, we knew that this unfortunate, untimely death was the will of God. That did not decrease the pain and sorrow, but it did help us through the situation. "Still Everything"[5] was the song that we chose for the homegoing service. A group from IBC – along with our children – sang it, and it was absolutely beautiful. Max would have been so proud. It was perfect to combine his children that he loved so deeply and IBC that he also loved with all of his heart and had such a love, compassion, and passion for the students that we had worked with throughout the years. The lyrics to that song are very moving. I still weep when I hear it and still believe in every word.

Angels:

I mentioned several times throughout this book about feeling the presence of angels and how that was not the everyday norm for me and how it brought me much comfort during the end of Max's life, his death, and the first months immediately after his passing.

The first occurrence was right at the time Max was diagnosed with liver cancer and we knew he was terminal without a divine miracle. We had gotten home from the hospital or a doctor's visit, I cannot remember for sure, and I was in the laundry room when I felt a touch on my back/shoulder area. I turned around thinking that one of my children or my mother had come in through the garage door and wanted me for something. I turned around to find that no one was there. I had a feeling come over me that let me know that it was God, He knew where I was, it was not going to be easy, but He had sent an angel to walk alongside me on this difficult journey.

The second occurrence was the night of Max's death when my daughter, Emily, and I were sound asleep and rose and sat up at the exact same time which was the time of Max's last breath. It was very early in the morning, and we were sound asleep at opposite ends of the bed. I believe it was an angel that swept through and was present at the time of Max's death. It was not a frightening thing – it was a beautiful, peaceful transition. During the next few months, I felt the presence of an angel several times at some of my darkest hours. Again, it was not frightening but very comforting. I feel honored and privileged that God was that close to my situation and my pain that He assured me I had comforting angels surrounding me. As I also mentioned previously, I found that I could not really talk much about this to individuals because they became overly concerned about me. I was in a very painful, distraught frame of mind, and I think those close to me were concerned that I was not coping well and may be having a mental health break, so I did not mention it anymore and just felt solace and comfort in the encounters.

Months later, a pastor's wife reached out to me by text. She said it may seem like a strange question, but did I see or feel angels at the time of Max's death. I texted her back and told her it was not strange at all and briefly told her what I had described above. I told her I did not talk about it because people were becoming concerned or thinking I was losing my mind, but I knew I was in the presence of an angel or angels at times, and it got me through my darkest days. She assured I was not losing my mind and then shared with me that the Wednesday evening, the week of Max's passing, their church had their children praying for us during their midweek children's church. They then drew cards to send to Max. I remember him receiving the cards, but I was so busy with the occurring events that I did not read them all. She sent me one from a young child that had a picture of only me (not Max) and there were angels surrounding me.

This was a confirmation that I "was not going crazy" and that I had, in fact, been surrounded by angels. I am so thankful she shared with me.

As I am entering my second year of grief, I am thankful for the God-given comfort I have had along this journey. I am not sure how I would have survived the last year without God, my family, my pastor, and church family that have walked with me on this rough and difficult journey. I know God will remain right alongside me as I continue to journey and embrace my new normal as a widow. Many times over the years I have discussed contentment with individuals in a time in their life that they wanted things to be different, to change, or a situation to be resolved. I always advised them to find contentment right where they were, continue to do what they knew was right, and God would work it all out. I am trying to follow my own advice as I move forward. I want to find contentment where I am – God will work it all out! Below are more scriptures that I found encouraging along the way.

> And the LORD, he it is that doth go before thee; He will be with thee, He will not fail thee, neither forsake thee: fear not, neither be dismayed.
> Deuteronomy 31:8

> The LORD shall fight for you, and ye shall hold your peace.
> Exodus 14:14

Trust in him at all times; ye people, Pour out your heart before him: God is a refuge for us. Selah.

Psalm 62:8

The LORD is my shepherd; I shall not want. He maketh me to lie down in green pastures: he leadeth me beside the still waters. He restoreth my soul: he leadeth me in the paths of righteousness for his name's sake. Yea, though I walk through the valley of the shadow of death, I will fear no evil: for thou art with me; thy rod and thy staff they comfort me. Thou preparest a table before me in the presence of mine enemies: thou anointest my head with oil; my cup runneth over. Surely goodness and mercy shall follow me all the days of my life: and I will dwell in the house of the LORD for ever.

Psalms 23

Endnotes

1—It Is Well With My Soul, Horatio Gates Spafford, 1873, public domain
2—Jireh
Elevation Music and Maverick City Music
3—Helping Someone in Grief, 17 Things You Need to Know, Anne Peterson, https://www.annepeterson.com/wp-content/uploads/2018/07/Helping-Someone-in-Grief-17-Things-You-Need-to-Know-processing-WITH-Memes.pdf
4—Never Walk Alone, Hope Darst, Released by: Fair Trade Services Release date: 4 November 2022 C-line: © 2022 Hope Darst under exclusive license to Fair Trade Services, LLC
5—Still Everything, Benita Jones, Integrity Music

www.ingramcontent.com/pod-product-compliance
Lightning Source LLC
Chambersburg PA
CBHW060856050426
42453CB00008B/990